Challenges from Narnia for Today

Messages from the seven Chronicles of Narnia
for life in the 21st Century

Ken Fitchew

"Are - are you there too, Sir?" said
Edmund.

"I am," said Aslan. "But there I have
another name. You must learn to know
me by that name. This was the very
reason why you were brought to Narnia,
that by knowing me here for a little, you
may know me better there."

(The Voyage of the Dawn Treader,
Chapter 16)

Clear Word

ISBN   0-9537816-1-5

First published in 2005 by Clear Word
25 Starfield Close, Ipswich IP4 5JQ United Kingdom
Email: publications@clear–word.co.uk

Icons for stories created by John Pinder

Contents

Preface

When I first read the Chronicles of Narnia, I enjoyed them as stories, but every now and then a line in the story would leap out at me, resonating with other things that I knew or was interested in. Often in just a sentence, buried in the story, I recognised a summary of a deep truth relevant to life today.

Although C.S. Lewis emphasised that the stories were not initially written as Christian allegories, nevertheless, in common with others, I found them reminding me of key Christian truths and portraying them in a way which helped them come alive.

In this booklet I have sought to list some of these key sentences that grabbed my attention, and to provide some links to their relevance to life in the twenty-first century, especially from the viewpoint of Christian belief. I have called them Challenges, since there is not much point in recognising a truth if we then do nothing about it. Of course, the links that I have made to the Christian faith and to life today must be my responsibility. I hope that readers of this booklet will also be inspired to read C.S. Lewis's other books to learn more of his own insights.

My aim is to encourage people to read the stories, and also to pause and think of ways in which they can be an inspiration to us for our lives today.

My thanks are due to a number of friends who have offered helpful comments on the draft. I would welcome any other comments that would help me to improve any later editions.

Ken Fitchew

Introduction

Stories for children and adults

Although written 50 years ago, the Chronicles of Narnia continue to find a readership who enjoy them. Although they are often thought of as children's stories, Lewis himself foresaw the interest that adults would have in them, as he indicated in the dedication of the first to be written, *The Lion, the Witch and the Wardrobe*, where he writes to Lucy Barfield "But some day you will be old enough to start reading fairy tales again." In his short essay entitled *Sometimes fairy stories may say best what is to be said*, Lewis says, "The inhibitions which I hoped my stories would overcome in a child's mind may exist in a grown-up's mind too, and may perhaps be overcome by the same means." (p.60 of Reference 1.) This essay provides a lot of insight into Lewis's view of his stories.

Values conveyed by the stories

One reason why the stories have remained popular with adults is because of the values and truths of human and spiritual life which they portray. The reader can recognise the attitudes of so many of the characters as reflecting human behaviour today, and the stories draw out the consequences of these different attitudes. However, Lewis denied that the stories had originally been designed to be Christian allegories. He said that they started with pictures in his imagination and grew from there. "At first there wasn't even anything Christian about them; that element pushed itself in of its own accord." (Ref 1, p.58). However, many readers will see the Lion Aslan, who, according to Lewis "came bounding into the story" and "pulled the whole story together" (Ref 1, p.64), as reflecting certain aspects of the person of Christ in both what he said and what he does.

C.S. Lewis's journey to faith

It was while Lewis was a tutor at Oxford University that he finally became a Christian, partly through the influence of friends such as

J.R.R. Tolkien, author of *The Lord of the Rings*. He described the key stages in his experience in his book *Surprised by Joy*. He later became a well-known author and apologist for Christian faith, with a gift for communicating clearly to ordinary people. This helps to explain why so many readers of the Chronicles of Narnia find that they reflect elements of Christian belief.

Some key themes

As mentioned above, the Narnia stories should not be considered as an exhaustive, self-consistent Christian allegory. We can also note that some aspects of life and human experience are missing from them (although it is remarkable how many are there in some form!). Those who enjoy the books also need to remember that they have no authority in themselves, so we should not be misled into thinking that because something happens in Narnia, there must be a clear parallel in our world.

However, there are a number of key Christian themes that many people see as pushing their way into one or more of the books.

- The creation of the world, the entry of evil into it, and its final end.

- The existence of a God, who established the world, and His Representative, who cared enough about the world to die for it, but who came alive again, conquering death, reminding us of Jesus Christ in Christian teaching.

- The Creator's personal intervention in the lives of individuals, seeking an individual relationship with each one, again reflecting God's attitude and revealed in Christ's behaviour as recorded in the Bible.

- The need to believe in Him, trust Him and follow Him closely, even at times when he seems distant.

The points are explained in a little more detail from the standpoint of Christian belief in the chapter at the end of this book.

Challenges

The following seven chapters of this book each relate to one of the Chronicles of Narnia. The Chronicles are presented in the order in which the story unfolds, although this differs from the order in which they were published. Each chapter starts with a brief reminder of the key events in that Chronicle. This is then followed by a number of reflections on what seem to me to be interesting and helpful challenges from the story. In each case I have used a key sentence from the actual story to anchor the thought, mainly because most of the challenges came to me through such sentences shouting at me that here was some quite deep truth for today. However, to really appreciate the point fully it is important to read the chapter of the relevant Chronicle to understand the context of the quotation.

Of course, these are the challenges as they strike me. It might be that my interpretation does not fit exactly with the beliefs that Lewis found "pushing themselves into the story". However, if they help the reader to pause and think, then I will be pleased. My hope is to encourage people to appreciate the ways in which such stories can be an inspiration to us and help us in developing our understanding of life, and in particular the message of Christ for individuals and society today.

Please read the books!

The sections in this book dealing with the different Chronicles are intended for people who have already read the relevant one of the seven Chronicles, since it is only by knowing the full context of the quotations used that the real challenges become apparent.

The Magician's Nephew

To remind you . . .

Polly and her friend Digory, whose mother is very ill, are tricked by Digory's Uncle Andrew into using magic rings to go to another World. They find themselves in Charn, where Digory stupidly wakes Jadis, the last Empress of Charn. When they return to Uncle Andrew's study, Jadis has come with them. When Jadis causes chaos in London, Digory and Polly manage to use their rings to get her back to the wood-between-the-worlds, along with a London cabby and his horse, but instead of returning Jadis to Charn, they all find their way into another world, which is empty, although not for long.

Soon they hear a voice singing, and with the song a whole living world is created in front of them. They then see the singer, a magnificent lion called Aslan. The new world is populated by many animals and other creatures, and Aslan chooses some to be talking animals. These are to be the population of this land of Narnia, and the Cabby and his wife are to be the first king and queen. Jadis runs away from Aslan, becoming the White Witch, bent on the destruction of Narnia.

Digory has had to confess to Aslan that it was his selfish attitude that had brought the White Witch to Narnia, and he and Polly are given a special task in order to protect Narnia from the White Witch. After completing this task, Aslan sends Uncle Andrew, Polly and Digory back to London, along with an apple which will bring healing to Digory's mother.

Finding an excuse

"We can't get out of it now. We shall always be wondering what else would have happened if we had struck the bell."

Digory had already fallen under the spell of the bell. He really wanted to know what would happen if he struck it, and so made this excuse (above) to continue in what he wanted to do, appealing to the inscription written beside the bell. Polly kept her head. She recognised the danger in the spell, and also knew that Digory was just being stubborn. He didn't need to know what would happen. Unfortunately Polly stopped reasoning clearly and simply escalated the quarrel, which led to the disastrous result of Digory striking the bell.

After first ignoring the warning on the inscription, Digory was very willing to refer to it when it suited him, since it gave him an excuse for doing what he wanted. However, as he admitted to Aslan later in the story, if he was really honest, he had only been pretending.

There are many situations in life where we know what we should do, but it is convenient to seize on any excuse that we can find to suggest that we are justified in doing what we want.

Awe at creation

"I'd ha' been a better man all my life if I'd known there were things like this."

The Cabby's reaction to hearing and seeing the creation of Narnia was one of awe, not just of the power displayed, but of the "goodness" of it all—his reaction was of wonder, not of terror. The amazing sights inspired him in a way which made him realise that his own life did not match up to the greatness displayed here. His attitude is maintained, as he witnesses more of creation unfolding, and then sees the Singer, the Creator, himself. A real appreciation of beauty in human art or music can be inspiring, but what the Cabby saw was living art and divine music, seen and heard in creation—the real performance, not a representation.

There is a "Wow!" factor in seeing creation, especially strong the first time one sees something new, like a distant snow-capped mountain range or a dramatic sunset, but which all too often becomes dulled with time. As with the Cabby, a real appreciation of the world should inspire us in a way which affects our attitudes and lifestyle, and the true basis of this is not creation itself, but the fact that it points to a Creator. If we really appreciate the wonder of life, we will look to the Creator and take note of how we can be, and already are, part of His revealed plan.

The commission—how to live

"Creatures, I give you yourselves," said the strong, happy voice of Aslan. "I give you forever this land of Narnia. I give you the woods, the fruits, the rivers. I give you the stars and I give you myself."

Aslan gave the talking animals their mandate—how they were to live. He gave them great things to enjoy. He continues by saying that the dumb animals were also theirs, but were to be treated with respect. True appreciation of the richness of the world we have been entrusted with will lead to care for creation, with no wish to exploit it.

He also gave them himself—a reminder that it was not just his power which had brought the world into being, but his presence and intervention that would be caring for the world throughout its existence. This echoes teaching that runs through the Bible, that God is not a remote Power, but is available and wanting to be part of our daily lives.

This great promise came with the warning—not to forget their calling and go back to the mechanical view of life of the dumb beasts. This is a picture of the emptiness that can result if people lose sight of their calling to serve Him who not only creates and sustains the laws of physics, but offers Himself as an essential ingredient of life as it should be lived.

Time for action

"I asked, are you ready?" said the Lion.

When Digory was asked by Aslan whether he was willing to undo the wrong that he had done to Aslan's country by bringing the Witch there, Digory started by say he didn't see how it was possible for him to undo it. Aslan was not interested in discussing what was possible—he was only asking Digory if he was prepared to act. Digory had to stop being limited by what he thought possible, and follow Aslan's directions, trusting that he had reasons that were bigger and deeper than Digory could even imagine.

There are times when we have done enough reasoning and considering, and action is required. In Digory's case, his job was not to understand all the details of the path ahead, but just to be willing to begin, in the confidence that Aslan knew what he was doing and the Digory was part of that plan.

For people who are really trying to follow God's plan for their lives, there may also be times to start moving, without waiting and holding back because we don't understand how everything will work out.

Suffering shared and understood

He [Digory] was very sad, and he wasn't even sure all the time that he had done the right thing; but whenever he remembered the shining tears in Aslan's eyes he became sure.

The witch had been tempting Digory to take a bite of an apple for himself, and also to take one for his mother. The subtle arguments had been persuasive, but in his heart he had known that this was wrong. At last he had had the strength to defy the witch. He faced a bitter struggle on the way home, knowing that he had turned down a possible means of helping his mother.

The one thing that reassured him was remembering the tears he had seen in Aslan's eyes when Digory had mentioned his mother. Although the Lion had promised nothing about healing his mother, he knew that Aslan understood and shared his pain. This was enough to reassure him.

Something that has encouraged Christians throughout the centuries is the fact that because He lived as a man on earth, Jesus can understand human life, including the difficult times of suffering and rejection. He who not only saw suffering but experienced it himself, understands all painful situations today.

The Lion, the Witch and the Wardrobe

To remind you . . .

While playing hide-and-seek at the house of Professor Kirk, Lucy hides in a wardrobe and finds that it leads into a completely different world, the land of Narnia, where it is always winter. Her brothers and sister, Peter, Edmund and Susan do not believe her. Edmund later also finds his way into Narnia, but does not admit this, because while there he has met the White Witch who is responsible for the sad state of Narnia. The White Witch has persuaded Edmund to try to bring all the children to Narnia, promising him good things, but actually so that she can destroy them.

When, later, the four children do all find their way into Narnia together, they meet some beavers who have been told to take them to see Aslan, the mighty Lion who first established Narnia. However, Edmund slips away to betray them to the White Witch.

It soon becomes obvious that with Aslan's return, the power of the White Witch has been broken, except that even Aslan has to admit that Edmund's treachery means that his life is forfeit. Aslan takes Edmund's place, so satisfying the ancient law, but death cannot hold him, and he comes alive again, leading the talking animals in defeating the White Witch. The four children are then established as kings and queens in Narnia, where they rule for a number of years of Narnian time before finding their way back through the wardrobe.

A will to change

"It isn't something I have done. I'm doing it now, this very moment."

Mr Tumnus had befriended Lucy for the purpose of handing her over to the White Witch. As he has got to know her over tea, he is convicted of how wrong the thing is that he is actually doing at that very moment.

It is one thing to be sorry for things we have done in the past or to make new resolutions about the future, but what about the present? It is much more difficult to change our hearts and minds when we are in the middle of something that we realise is wrong, but Mr Tumnus gives us an example of real openness to change. He became uncomfortable about what he was doing, and in spite of the cost and risk to himself, he decided to do what was right and helped Lucy go back home. His decision was not about doing the right thing some time in the future—for Mr Tumnus the time to change was *now*. In fact, as we learn later, his right decision did cost him a lot, but it was also the first step which moved him from the service of the White Witch to being a true follower of Aslan.

There are times when we need to listen to our conscience and respond—not some time in the future, but now!

Open to truth?

"But how do you know," he [the Professor] said, "that your sister's story is not true?"

Peter and Susan were trying to reconcile Lucy's story with reality as they knew it. They could not understand how the back of the wardrobe could sometimes lead to a magical country and sometimes not. They were trying to understand everything in terms of what they knew—their experience to date. The professor's question caused them to think more widely.

What we have been taught at school or by our friends or read in the newspapers may not actually reflect all there is to life. Just because something does not fit into our experience up till now does not mean that it cannot be true. If Peter and Susan refused to believe that there could be another country, they were actually believing that Lucy was either deluded or a liar, and neither of these explanations was any more satisfactory than the belief that she was speaking the truth.

The popular assumption that we are just machines and the universe came into being by chance may not actually be any more satisfactory than the view that the universe was created by Someone who is big enough to be outside time and space, and yet interested enough in people share with them something of his personality.

What is He like?

" 'Course he isn't safe. But he's good."

Mr and Mrs Beaver were telling the children about Aslan, the Son of the Emperor-beyond-the-Sea. They had just learned that he is a lion, and that sounds scary, so they wanted reassurance that he couldn't harm them. Mr Beaver tells them that he is not safe, but he's good, so anything that Aslan does will be for the best.

We all like to know that we are safe, and by this we mean that our expectations and comfort won't be upset. But God may have plans that do upset our lives; He may do things that we did not ask for and did not want. But we can have confidence that He is good.

Often the only way to make progress in our lives is for our comfortable pattern to be upset, and we may not like it. But if we have confidence in the goodness of God and his real love and care and concern for us, then we can look beyond these disturbances and rejoice in knowing, trusting and following Him who has good plans that go beyond our understanding and expectations.

A truer perspective

*All the things he [Edmund] had said to make himself believe
... sounded to him silly now.*

Edmund's selfish streak, which wanted him to be more important
than Peter, Susan and Lucy had resulted in him convincing
himself that he could believe the White Witch's promises. He had
now begun to realise, belatedly, that they had been false
promises—he had been deceived, first by the Witch and then by
himself!

We can all be deceived by only listening to what we want to hear.
We need to listen and respond to situations not just with our
emotions, but with our minds. However, in this chapter the first
glimmer of light appears when Edmund begins to realise his
mistake.

The first step in getting out of any such mess is to admit that we
are wrong. This is so much against human pride that it can be
hard, but the concept runs throughout the whole Bible. Pride in
our own ability is one of the biggest barriers to admitting we need
help from God. However, as we learn later, Edmund's life and
attitude could be turned around, and here was the first step on
that path towards recovery.

New life brings complete change

"This is no thaw," said the Dwarf, suddenly stopping. "This is Spring."

The White Witch has kept the land of Narnia in perpetual Winter, a Winter not even relieved by the happiness of Christmas. Now, in the light of overwhelming evidence, even the Witch's assistant has to admit that the old order is coming to an end.

This event was big—a real ending of the ice age, not because of a natural cycle, but because Aslan had come and his presence was changing the world. Even the Witch's dwarf recognised this truth. There is good news, and it is something to recognise and be excited about. The foretaste of Spring was soon to be endorsed by the ultimate defeat of the White Witch.

The good news of new life is something big and exciting. It is not just a way of improving the current situation a bit, but it brings the potential for the defeat of evil. According to Christian teaching, the coming of Christ in history, remembered especially at Christmas, was not just to provide some teaching on how to improve the social order, but to bring a completely new way of life, made possible only by trusting in Him.

The cost of redemption

"All shall be done," said Aslan. "But it may be harder than you think."

Lucy appealed to Aslan to save Edmund from the consequences of being a traitor and following the Witch. Aslan's reply was reassuring, but it only hinted at the cost that it was going to involve for him—eventually costing him his life.

This echoes the story at the centre of the Bible, that Jesus had to die in the place of others, in order to provide a way for all people to be delivered from spiritual death. According to the accounts in the gospels, Christ's disciples also found it hard to believe that the new life that He brought would be at the cost of His own life. This was going to be the ultimate example of love, but also the way to freedom and victory.

Fundamental laws

"Work against the Emperor's Magic?"

The Witch has told everyone that Edmund's life is forfeit because of his treachery. She has a right to his life, according to the fundamental principles upon which Narnia had been established by the Emperor-beyond-the-Sea. In order to save Edmund, Susan asks Aslan if he cannot do something to counteract this rule, only to find that Aslan would not hear of it.

This touches upon the Christian understanding of the world as God created it—not the physical world, but the spiritual laws behind it. Our wrong attitudes and actions have an inevitable consequence of spiritual death—eternal separation from the Creator. No clever schemes of our making can bypass such consequences. If there is to be a solution, it will be in accordance with those principles, not by overturning them. In Narnia, it would be a solution whereby Aslan saw that the principles were satisfied by offering his own life—a reminder of the death of Jesus as the ultimate and final sacrifice for all of us.

Victory over death

". . . death itself would start working backwards."

After seeing him killed, Susan and Lucy cannot believe it when they see Aslan alive again. He explains the deeper principles that the White Witch did not know of, that when he, being innocent, was killed in Edmund's place, he would not only free Edmund but also provide victory over death.

This reminds us of the central point of the Christian faith—the resurrection of Jesus. Accepting Jesus just as a good teacher misses the most important point. It was his action in dying and rising that provided the way to real freedom from the evil that had entered the world and led to death. It was only when Jesus followers saw him alive again that they understood truly what he had done for them and for everyone.

Priorities in using gifts

"Daughter of Eve," said Aslan in a graver voice, "others are at the point of death. Must **more** *people die for Edmund?"*

Edmund had been wounded in the battle, and Lucy had administered some of her cordial to heal him. She was waiting to see the result. Aslan was calling her to move on, to stop worrying about Edmund, since there were others who needed her healing cordial.

What Lucy had done in healing Edmund was good, but she was getting distracted from doing more. She had been given the gift of the cordial, not just to heal Edmund, but anyone who was in need of healing.

It is possible to get so wrapped up in one thing (even a good thing), that we neglect to use the gifts that we have been given to the full, to help others in need.

Consistent faith

"One day you'll see him, and another you won't."

Mr Beaver was commenting on the fact that Aslan had slipped away from the celebrations at Cair Paravel. Although they depended on Aslan, there would be times when he was not visibly with them. They had to continue to live without his immediate presence and guidance.

There may be times in our lives of spiritual revelation, when things seem clear to us, and we are confident of God's presence and leading and guidance in what we do. But there may be other times when we have to carry on without that direct encouragement. The real test of character, faith and commitment is pressing on in doing what is right and trusting, even when things are hard. This is a recurring theme in the Narnia stories— faithfulness in holding to the truth despite lack of visible evidence. Real faith and trust is shown in the hard times when we do not feel the immediate inspiration and emotional support of God's presence in a real way, and when God actually feels a long way off, or even non-existent.

The Horse and his Boy

To remind you . . .

Shasta is a young boy who lives in the land of Calormen. He lives with and works for a fisherman who Shasta believes is his father but who had actually found Shasta as a baby and brought him up to work for him. When a Calormene Tarkaan passes and demands accommodation for the night, Shasta overhears him bargaining with the fisherman to buy him as a slave. The Tarkaan's horse, a captured Narnian horse called Bree, suggests to Shasta that they run away to Narnia together. During their journey north, they are chased by a Lion, and as a result meet up with a Calormene girl, Aravis, and another talking horse, Hwin, who are also fleeing to Narnia.

In passing through the city of Tashbaan, Shasta becomes separated from the others, and learns that a royal party from Narnia, who are visiting Tashbaan, are in danger, but have a plan to escape. Aravis, meanwhile, finds out that the escape has been successful, but that as a result the Calormene Prince Rabadash plans to invade Narnia and Archenland. When Aravis, Shasta and the horses all meet up, they cross the desert to go to Archenland and Narnia, to warn of the impending attack.

When they arrive, Shasta finds King Lune of Archenland in time to warn him to prepare for the attack. During this last part of their adventures, all four of the travellers meet Aslan, the Lion, and learn how he has been looking after them throughout their journey. Shasta finds out his own true identity, and learns that his role in saving Archenland had been foretold long before.

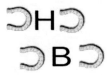

Inner longings

"They were only the Tisroc's wars, and I fought in them as a slave and dumb beast. Give me the Narnian wars where I shall fight as a free Horse among my own people."

Shasta has been interested to know about Bree's experiences, but Bree is not interested in talking about them. Although Bree has not yet met Aslan, and he has much to learn, in his heart he longs for something different. He knows he has been trapped in a life which is not where he belongs, serving ambitions which are futile.

One of the key questions in life is what we are here for. It is possible to get so entrapped in the day-to-day business of life that we lose sight of the most important things. For a Christian, the right sort of ambition, to use our lives and the gifts given to us effectively in doing things which are after God's heart, is something to be nurtured.

Does it matter what people think?

"Well," said Hwin humbly (she was a very sensible mare), "the main thing is to get there."

The best plan that they had for getting through Tashbaan would require disguise, involving Bree having his tail cut in an untidy manner. His immediate reaction was that he wanted to look his best when he arrived in Narnia, so the idea of having his tail cut did not appeal. Hwin pointed out the obvious—his appearance was not as important as getting there. Bree was letting a trivial point of what people thought of him threaten their whole project.

Most of us find it really hard not to always present ourselves in the best possible light, justifying our actions at the least sight of criticism. Hwin's common sense, even if a boring and unwelcome message, is that sometimes to achieve what we want most we have to swallow our pride, perhaps even leaving criticism unanswered in order to achieve a greater goal.

This can apply especially to those seeking to follow Christ. To really live for Him and achieve His purposes in our lives may sometimes require ignoring what people think of us, or even our 'rights', if these get in the way of achieving what really matters.

When it's tough

He [Shasta] had not yet learned that if you do one good deed your reward usually is to be set to do another and harder and better one.

Shasta and the others had just arrived, after being chased by a lion, and Shasta might well have been looking for a short rest. But the Hermit tells him that he must press on immediately if their task is to be accomplished. This was a call to perseverance in achieving the task that they had to do.

In facing the difficult issues and battles of life, there are times when an urgent situation leaves no scope of sitting back and reflecting on how things are going. In fact those who have just achieved something are often the ones who are in the best (even the only) position to do something else that needs doing. It does seem unfair, but 'fairness' does not come into it if we are serving and obeying Someone we acknowledge as Lord. Shasta had not yet met Aslan to know him, but he recognised what his duty was.

Who are You?

"One who has waited long for you to speak."

The is the answer that Shasta got when he at last had the courage to ask the invisible being walking beside him "Who are you?" Of course it turns out to be Aslan. As Shasta learns, it is Aslan who has been looking after him and the others throughout their journey. It was he who had first brought Shasta, Bree, Aravis and Hwin together, and he who had looked after them since, and indeed he who, years before, had pushed the boat holding the baby Shasta to the shore, so that he was not drowned.

We may think that we have been unfortunate in some things that have happened to us. But the message is that there is One who is waiting to listen to us as soon as we are willing to genuinely admit that we need help. But it will have to be help on His terms, not ours. Just as Shasta's journey led him to realise that he had a place in Aslan's plan, so it is up to us to find the place that God has for us in his plan, not to ask Him to help us fulfil out ambitions.

When Shasta asks a second time, "Who are you?" the answer he gets is "Myself." It is not for us to expect to really understand everything about God, but to accept Him as He is, and rejoice that He wants a relationship with us. There is a time to stop trying to sort out our lives on our own, and seek a relationship with the One who loves us and wants us to trust Him for the future.

Real devotion!

"Please," she said, "you're so beautiful. You can eat me if you like."

Hwin's response on seeing Aslan was one of such awe and attraction that she said she'd rather be eaten by Aslan than fed by anyone else.

Of course Aslan didn't want to eat Hwin, but the picture reflects the ultimate attitude of devotion! Hwin was so overwhelmed by Aslan that she didn't even care about her life. All she was interested in was serving Aslan in any way he wanted.

This is true worship in which the worshipper is so overwhelmed by the greatness of his or her Lord that ambitions and even life itself count for nothing. This is the sort of devotion that causes people to leave secure, well-paid jobs or give up hobbies, in order to have time to do what they believe God would have them do. This is the type of call that Jesus gave to people to follow Him.

Facing up to ourselves

"Aslan," said Bree in a shaken voice, "I'm afraid I must be rather a fool."

Bree had been telling Aravis that Aslan was the Lion who had delivered Narnia from the White Witch, but when asked if he was a real Lion, Bree denied it, saying it would be disrespectful to think of him as such—the term was just a metaphor, a picture. Then Aslan appears, and Bree realises that his previous philosophising has missed the point—Aslan is real!

It is possible to have a system of beliefs which is just theoretical, perhaps even based on stories that we consider were not literally true, although they have significant meaning. However, the Christian faith is not based on theories and metaphors, however helpful they may be, but on a relationship with a real Personality, who has revealed himself in history. Jesus called people to believe in Him, not as a set of abstract concepts, but as God's revelation in a real person.

Prince Caspian

To remind you . . .

Peter, Susan, Edmund and Lucy find themselves suddenly pulled into the land of Narnia, where they had been kings and queens long before, having been appointed by Aslan, the Lion. They meet Trumpkin the dwarf, who tells them that Caspian, the true young king of Narnia, and the loyal talking animals with him, are being attacked by Caspian's Uncle Miraz. Caspian had been brought up by Miraz, but he recently had to flee when he heard that Miraz wanted to kill him. During his flight, Caspian had for the first time met the talking animals, who he had heard of, but whose existence Miraz had always denied. Trumpkin had come to look for help, not because he believed that the children existed, but out of loyalty to Caspian.

The children, together with Trumpkin, go to help Caspian in his fight against Miraz. On the way, they all meet Aslan, the Lion. The dwarf learns that Aslan really does exist, and the others all learn more of how to trust and follow him. When they arrive, their first job is to deliver Caspian from some traitors who are encouraging him to use evil powers to win the battle. Peter and the others then confront Miraz and his supporters. Aslan appears again, bringing freedom to those who have been oppressed by the regime of Miraz, and Caspian is restored to his rightful place as king.

Truths neglected and suppressed

"It was you Telmarines who silenced the beasts and the trees and the fountains . . . and are now trying to cover up even the memory of them."

Dr Cornelius is explaining to Caspian that the old stories of the rich life in Narnia, with talking animals and dwarfs, were true. It is Caspian's race which wishes to suppress the truth about them, because the Telmarines took over the land from them, and wish to deny the fact that they existed.

We hear at times of extreme regimes where "the party line" is taught incessantly, with no opportunity being allowed for anyone to check its truth. However, sometimes, in milder form, this can occur closer to home, and we need all to be on our guard to assess correctly the latest ideas that are thrown at us, whether as teaching from politicians or those in authority, or just by pressure from our peers or the media.

This message can be applied to Christian belief today. Just because something is laughed at and despised by the vast majority of people does not necessarily mean that it is not true. There may be reasons why a society does not wish to face up to certain truths, and the simplest way of doing this is to deny and ridicule them.

A lonely path?

"I couldn't have left the others and come up to you alone, how could I? ...Oh well, I suppose I could. Yes, and it wouldn't have been alone, I know, not if I was with you."

Lucy had tried to encourage the others to follow Aslan, but in the end she had gone along with them—in the opposite direction to the way she knew Aslan wanted them to go. Aslan is now challenging her with a really hard lesson and a hard task. First, she learns that she should have followed Aslan regardless of what the others said and done. The quotation is Lucy's response as she accepts the truth.

However, now Aslan was giving her a second chance, asking her to follow this through. Lucy was learning that real devotion, trust and obedience to him can mean walking a lonely path. But actually it is not a matter of being totally alone since the one who matters most to her would be with her.

There is a clear parallel here for those who are seeking to follow Christ. He warned that those who really want to follow Him will be in a minority, and the road will be hard, but he also promised his presence.

Keeping focused—eyes fixed on Aslan

Lucy went first, biting her lip and trying not to say all the things she thought of saying to Susan. But she forgot them when she fixed her eyes on Aslan.

Lucy had good reason for being upset with Susan, who had been so negative and unsupportive. If she had dwelt on this, her thoughts would have festered, and she would have got more and more bitter and resentful.

She found the best way to counter this resentment was to look ahead and concentrate on the task of following Aslan. This made the negative thoughts fade away until she forgot them.

Resentment and anger may arise easily, especially when our ambitions are thwarted by others. However, both the teaching and the example of Jesus show that this is not the way. A powerful encouragement to his followers is to be found in remembering how He put up with the most extreme form of 'unfair' treatment, and rejoicing that they have been called to follow him.

Just do it!

"You three, you sons of Adam and son of Earth, hasten into the Mound and deal with what you will find there."

Aslan, having revealed himself to them all, told Peter, Edmund and Trumpkin to get on with the job in hand. He didn't give them exact instructions, but just told them to deal with the situation.

We have been given skills and abilities and minds to use. There are times when we are not told exactly how to do something, but just to do it. And some jobs need tackling fast—there is no time to hang back for endless debate on to the best approach. When the entered the Mound they found they arrived at the crucial moment.

There are times when those who claim to be followers of Christ need this sort of encouragement. If we have been given gifts and opportunities, then it is up to us to get on and use them.

Qualities for leadership

"If you had felt yourself sufficient, it would have been a proof that you were not."

Caspian, like Solomon of old, felt ill-equipped to be king, realising that he was completely lacking in experience. However, he was willing to take on the task assigned to him. So often today, leaders are expected to be totally competent people who have all the answers at their fingertips, are confident in their ability to handle every situation, and have a good image on TV. Aslan's words remind us of the dangers of this attitude.

The tasks of leadership are not to be taken on lightly, but with a due awareness of the difficulties and responsibilities involved. Nonetheless, feeling inadequate is not an excuse for avoiding responsibility. Caspian was willing to take on the role that was right for him, and that only he could do effectively.

Who are we?

"You come of the Lord Adam and the Lady Eve," said Aslan. "And that is both honour enough to erect the head of the poorest beggar, and shame enough to bow the shoulders of the greatest emperor on earth."

This is Aslan's reply to Caspian, who has said he is ashamed of his ancestry (pirates and invaders), and it provides two challenges about our attitudes to ourselves.

On the one hand, every human can be proud of being descended from Adam and Eve who were, according the Bible, the first to be made "in the image of God." As such, whatever, our shortcomings or our situation, we have reason to see ourselves, and every other human, as of value before God. We can be proud, not of what we have done, but of the fact that we have a job to do in living for Him.

However, because of our fallen human nature, we all do wrong, and this means that none of us, not even the wisest, the most skilful, the most popular or the most powerful has any reason to be proud of our accomplishments. We need to be continuously aware of our weaknesses, our smallness and our dependence on God's grace.

The Voyage of the Dawn Treader

To remind you . . .

Edmund and Lucy are looking at a picture of a ship at sea when their disagreeable cousin, Eustace, joins them. As they look at the picture, they all find themselves falling into the sea, and are taken on board by their old friend Caspian, King of Narnia, who is undertaking a voyage to find seven lost Lords. In a number of adventures, visiting many islands they succeed in tracking down all the lost lords, either finding them, or else finding evidence of where they had perished. On Dragon Island, Eustace finally meets the Lion, Aslan, whom all the others know already, and as a result is dramatically changed.

They have many adventures, on several occasions learning more of Aslan's watching over them and plan for them. More of the wonders of Aslan's land are explained to them by Ramandu and his daughter, and the ambition of Reepicheep, the mouse, to get there at any cost is strengthened.

Caspian and the others continue journeying east until they reach the end of the ocean as they know it. For Caspian it is time to return, but the three children and Reepicheep continue as far as they can. Reepicheep then goes on alone, while the children again encounter Aslan, who explains more about how they can know him in their own world before sending them back.

Serving in word only

"Does he [Governor Grumpas] still acknowledge the King of Narnia for his lord?"

"In words, yes. All is done in the King's name. But he would not be best pleased to find a real, live king of Narnia coming in upon him."

King Caspian has come to the Lone Islands unannounced, and is asking Lord Bern whether the Governor of the Lone Islands, Grumpas, will acknowledge him as king. The quotation includes Bern's reply.

There are two ways of acknowledging someone as Lord of our lives, controlling our conduct and hearts. One is with willing, whole-hearted devotion, based on a relationship of respect and love. The other is with just in name, a cursory nod to the appropriate words, but without a willing heart behind it. As is shown in the case of Grumpas, a nominal allegiance does not lead to real service, and so does not welcome the reality of the presence of the true Lord.

The New Testament speaks of the challenge to be ready for an unexpected encounter with Christ, either on his return or as a result of the day-to-day uncertainty of life for all of us.

The futility of anger

He [Eustace] could get even with Caspian and Edmund now—But the moment he thought this, he realised that he didn't want to. He wanted to be friends.

Eustace's thoughts had been full of resentment, bitterness and the desire for revenge against Lucy, Edmund, Caspian, Reepicheep, and probably almost everyone else on the *Dawn Treader*. Now, having become a dragon, he has the power to act. But the truth was dawning in his mind: the path of anger and revenge is a path of loneliness, cutting one off from the friendship of others, and in his heart Eustace realises that deep down this is not what he wants.

Revenge and retaliation may bring a sense of satisfaction, but all that is satisfied is the spirit of bitterness which has been harboured. Worse still, brooding in this way builds that spirit in a way destroys the ability for positive relationships. It is good to be open to recognise the signs of this, without waiting for such a hard lesson as Eustace had.

We can't change ourselves

"Then the lion said—but I don't know if it spoke—'You will have to let me undress you.'"

Eustace is here telling Edmund what happened to him when he met Aslan. Aslan had told Eustace to undress before he could bathe. Eustace tried, and shed three dragon skins, but it didn't make any difference—he was still a dragon. It was then that Eustace realised that he would have to let the lion undress him.

When people realise that their lives are in a mess, the first instinct is to try and sort it out themselves. But there are some things in our lives that we cannot do.

A message running through the Bible is that we need to give up on our own efforts to sort our lives out, and allow help from outside. That help may be painful, as Eustace found as Aslan removed the last dragon skin, but once we submit to it, it is effective, and changes us from the inside, not just the outside.

Knowing God

"But who is Aslan? Do you know him?"

"Well—he knows me," said Edmund. "He's the great lion, the son of the Emperor-beyond-the-Sea, who saved me and saved Narnia."

Eustace was asking Edmund whether he knew Aslan, and Edmunds reply is not quite what Eustace expected. Edmund did know Aslan, and the whole basis for this relationship was the fact that Aslan had actually died to save Edmund from the White Witch, as we read in *The Lion, the Witch and the Wardrobe*.

But Edmund's answer also shows that he knew that he could never claim to know and understand Aslan in the same way that Aslan knew him, and it was Aslan's knowing him that mattered.

This exchange has some quite deep meaning for Christians. It is true that Christians can say that they know God, since they have learned about Him and experienced Him changing their lives and attitudes. But God is so great that no one can say they really know and understand Him. However, the other side of the coin is that God is big enough to know all about us, our experiences, strengths and failings, joys and sorrows, and that gives greater comfort than is possible by our saying that we understand Him.

Knowing or believing

"You can't know," said the girl. "You can only believe—or not."

Edmund had told Ramandu's daughter that his whole instinct was to believe what she said, but that he wanted to know how he could be certain that what she said was true. The answer was simple—he couldn't know for sure in that way. But he could take a step of faith, trusting that what his heart and mind told him was true. If he didn't do this, he would be choosing not to trust.

Reepicheep was the first to take this step forward, drinking the wine, believing the girl when she said this was from Aslan and would bring refreshment and no harm.

A similar situation may be experienced by those wanting to come to know about God, and in particular the person of Jesus, God's revelation to us. We may be seeking definite proof and evidence, but that can only take us so far. There comes a point where, in the light of the evidence that we have got, we can only say, "My heart tells me that it rings true. I am going to believe." When that point comes, Ramandu's daughter quietly warns us of the alternative. We must choose to believe—or not to believe.

Duty or privilege?

*A good many who had been anxious enough to **get** out of the voyage felt quite differently about being **left** out of it.*

Caspian and the others had taken on the crew for a particular purpose. He did not have the right to force them to continue after finding the lost Lords. His plan to encourage them to continue, involved helping them see things in a new light.

The right to participate in the final stage of the outward voyage was not to be seen as an extra duty being asked of them, but as an extra privilege being offered them. Did they really want to be known in the future as those who were offered a great opportunity and turned it down?

Our attitudes to many tasks are greatly influenced by how we view them, and it is all too easy to lose sight of the real value. Is homework just a duty to be done or an opportunity to learn and so be better able to help others in the future? Do we see bringing up children as a chore, or a great privilege in shaping the next generation of the world's population?

For the Christian, there is also a specific lesson from these words. Do we still see following Christ as a privilege and opportunity to jump at, or as a set of rules we must follow?

The Silver Chair

To remind you . . .

Eustace and Jill Pole are trying to escape from some bullies at their school, when they find themselves in a pleasant open woodland by a cliff. During an argument, Eustace falls over the cliff, but immediately a Lion appears and blows him far away. Jill has to meet the Lion, Aslan, and after admitting what she has done, is given a task for them both. She and Eustace are to seek the missing prince Rilian, son of the aged King Caspian. Aslan gives Jill four signs to follow.

They are helped on their way, first by some Owls, and then by Puddleglum, the marsh-wiggle, who accompanies them. They get distracted from the signs, especially after meeting the Green Lady, accompanied by a knight, and nearly fall prey to some giants to whom she directed them. Back on course, they end up in the depths of the earth and are captured by Earthmen who take them to see the Queen of the Underworld. Since she is absent they meet the knight who is very friendly, and explains that each day he must be bound to a silver chair, for an hour, while he suffers from a fit of madness. They face a final test, when the last sign suggests that the fit of madness is not what it seems.

Having found the lost prince, they realise that his disappearance is part of a plot against the land of Narnia, and find their way back to Narnia in time for Rilian to be united with his father, just before the old king dies. They also learn that death in Narnia is only a way into Aslan's country for King Caspian.

No other river

"If you're thirsty, you may drink."

A thirsty Jill was invited to drink by the Lion, who had just blown Eustace to safety. The only problem was that to have her thirst quenched would mean trusting Aslan, and she would rather not have had to face him. She tried bargaining, but was told that she had no other option. Somehow she knew that what the Lion said was true, and her only way of getting a drink was to take a step which would involve trusting him.

A key message of the Christian faith is that the way to Life starts with an encounter with Jesus; there is no other way. And this encounter can only be on His terms—no bargaining is possible. But those who take this step are not disappointed, and Jesus described the life that He offers as living water.

Who called who?

"You would not have called me unless I had been calling to you."

Had Eustace and Jill called for Aslan, or had Aslan called them? Both were true. The children had seen their need for deliverance from their miserable life at the school, but it was Aslan who had taken the first initiative—their action had been a response to his call.

The two sides of the coin are both present in the teaching of the Bible—God's initiative in calling individuals to follow him, and the need for us to admit our need to ask for help.

It is not very helpful to get hung up on theological debates as to whether we call for help on our own initiative or have been prompted to do so by God Himself. The important thing is that communication is established, opening the way for a new relationship. The fact that God calls us to be part of his plan is a tremendous motive to both rejoice and respond.

Who is in control?

"There are no accidents. Our guide is Aslan;"

Eustace and Jill had believed that the words UNDER ME had been put to guide them, but Rilian, in his enchanted state, had given another explanation—that these words were just part of an ancient inscription. Eustace and Jill's confidence had been shaken—perhaps they had not been led as they had thought.

It was Puddleglum who brought them back to reality. If they were following Aslan, and obeying him, then nothing that happened was an accident—it was all part of his plan.

When things seem to go wrong in life, the truth that Christians can fall back on is that if we are really seeking to follow what God wants, as revealed in Jesus, then somehow all things can work together for good.

Is it the sign?

"Aslan didn't tell Pole what would happen. He only told her what to do."

The party were now being more careful. They had resolved not to untie the Kinght from his chair, even if he begged them to do it. But now the Knight had given the final sign, by calling on them in Aslan's name.

It was Puddleglum's solid faith that helped them through this difficult decision. Should they stick to their resolution not to listen to the Prince, a resolution made with the best intentions of wisdom available to them at the time, or cast reason aside and simply trust in the signs. Puddleglum had no doubts that following Aslan meant doing what he said, even in a situation which was totally different from any they had imagined. This was the ultimate test of whether they were going to trust Aslan and the signs that he had given them, or whether they were going to 'interpret' these signs through the filter of their own wisdom.

Aslan had warned them that the signs would not appear as they expected them to. In the Christian life, a real test of faith and obedience is holding to what is right even when all human wisdom might point to the contrary.

Whatever happens . . .

"Whether we live or die, Aslan will be our good lord."

The party were escaping through the tunnel from the depths of the earth, when the lights went out and they were in utter darkness. Rilian, freed from his enchantment, was now the one to encourage the others with his constant faith in Aslan. Rilian was not sure that they would escape, but he was sure that it did not matter too much whether they lived or died as long as Aslan was in charge of their lives.

This attitude to life (and death) is one based on true trust and commitment. Many Christians find their faith tested at some point, often in a way not of their choosing, and reach a point where they have to admit they are not in control of events. It is at this point that true faith is revealed—accepting that whatever happens, it is sufficient to know that our hearts are set on serving Christ.

On guard

"And the lesson of it all is, Your Highness," said the oldest Dwarf, "that those Northern Witches always mean the same thing, but in every age they have a different plan for getting it."

This was the second time that a witch had sought to take over Narnia. The White Witch of the earlier generations had been replaced by the Green Lady. The words of the dwarf to Prince Rilian remind us that each generation needs to be on its guard against influences that will divert people from the truth.

As culture, society, politics, technology and other influences change, so the opportunities for people to be deceived also change. Those who are seeking the truth need to be on their guard against each set of new influences that arises.

To put it more positively, for Christians, each generation needs to consider how the unchanging truths about God's plan and revelation through Jesus can be related to and communicated to, the world they are living in.

The end and beginning of life

"Yes," said the Lion in a very quiet voice, almost (Jill thought) as if he were laughing. "He [Caspian] has died. Most people have, you know. Even I have. There are very few who haven't."

Caspian had died in Narnia, and now was alive again. The Lion had had his paw pierced with a thorn, and a drop of his blood had brought Caspian to life, in Aslan's country, with a new body, free from the limitations of old age.

Aslan did not comment directly on the fact that it was through the shedding of his blood that this change took place in Caspian, a reminder for Christians that death is only conquered through Jesus' death. But he went on to remind Eustace and Jill that death is not something to be afraid of. From Aslan's perspective, outside time and thinking of earlier generations throughout history, he could see that most people who have ever lived have experienced death already! More importantly, Eustace and Jill could be reassured by the fact that he had experienced it himself, referring to his death in *The Lion, the Witch and the Wardrobe*.

The fact that Jesus experienced death, and then met his followers after his resurrection, is perhaps the most reassuring thought for those who fear death today.

The Last Battle

To remind you . . .

When Shift, the ape, sees the skin of a dead lion in a pool, he persuades the donkey Puzzle to wear it. Shift plans to pretend that Puzzle is Aslan, the ruler behind Narnia, and so to control the land and its inhabitants, ruling it together with the Calormenes. Shift keeps Puzzle in a stable, only showing him briefly, lest the truth be discovered. The deceit is convincing, and results in King Tirian being taken captive. Tirian calls to Aslan for help, and this results in Eustace and Jill coming from the human world.

They free Puzzle, but the deceit spreads, and they can not convince all the other inhabitants of Narnia. The ape and the Calormene leader declare that Aslan and the Calormene god Tash are the same.

A number of the loyal animals join Tirian, Eustace and Jill for the last battle, which centres around what is in the stable—the true Aslan, Tash, or something else. During the fighting, many pass through the stable door, but when this happens to Tirian and the others, they find themselves in Aslan's country.

The time has come for the end of Narnia. All the remaining inhabitants have to face Aslan, and their reaction reflects their fate. As the Friends of Narnia appreciate the greatness of Aslan's land, and find that it encompasses all the good things from the past in a renewed and far better form, they realise that they have actually died in their own world, and are now experiencing the first taste of heaven, with Aslan, or Christ, for ever.

Manipulation and deceit

"Oh, well, of course, if you put it that way," said Puzzle.

Shift the ape is a master of manipulation when dealing with a simple, honest character like Puzzle. Not only does he use outright lies, but what is more dangerous because it is less obvious, he distorts the truth by providing alternative explanations and ideas at every turn. Although Puzzle is not really convinced by Shift's arguments, he does not know how to counter them.

Unless we have a clear view of what is right, we are vulnerable to distorted thinking. Often the attitudes and views presented in the media, soaps, etc, are made to appear plausible, especially when presented by someone who has an attractive personality, and in the presence of 'peer pressure', where we fear ridicule if we adopt a different attitude. We need to be on our guard to continually test these values and attitudes before we automatically go along with them.

The issue which Shift questioned was the character of Aslan. The deceit would shortly take a new twist with the ape saying that Aslan and Tash are one, reminding us of another popular and "politically correct" idea—that all religions are the same. Will we go along with the spirit of the age, or think and seek the truth?

Beyond Christmas

"Yes," said Queen Lucy. "In our world too, a stable once had something inside it that was bigger than our whole world."

In passing through the stable door, Tirian and the others had been amazed to find a new world, bigger and much more wonderful that the one they had left.

While slowly beginning to appreciate how great this new world was, Lucy reflects on the parallel in her world, the real world of humans. The Christmas story of a child born in a stable is remarkable only because of who the child was—one who is not only worshipped by the shepherds, wise men and others, but who is described later by his followers as one who made the world.

The coming of God as a man, Christ, to provide a way of salvation is the fundamental point of Christian truth, without which it all falls apart. While the celebration of Christmas has now become so commercialised as to be often unrecognisable, the central event of a baby born in a stable 2000 years ago is still cause for wonder and contemplation, as Lucy reminds us.

Self-imposed blindness

"You see," said Aslan. "They will not let us help them. They have chosen cunning instead of belief. Their prison is only in their own minds, yet they are in that prison; and so afraid of being taken in that they cannot be taken out."

When the dwarfs had been freed by Tirian and the others, they had decided on a course of action for which they were now reaping the harvest. They had decided to trust no one, and just to look after themselves and their own interests. Their answer to not being taken in by false truth was to deny that there was any greater power at all. They had followed this through in attacking both the talking horses and the Calormenes. But their refusal to believe in something greater than themselves was now making them incapable of recognising the truth, and of receiving the fantastic life that could be theirs if only they would accept it.

A term used in the Bible is of people "hardening their hearts", and this is used as a warning. Although God's offer of forgiveness and acceptance and new life is always open, continual rejection of the truth and focusing on self can make it increasingly difficult to respond.

Judgement or choice?

But as they came right up to Aslan one or other of two things happened to each of them. They all looked straight in his face.

The final separation came, of those who were Aslan's animals, dwarfs, etc, and those who weren't. Those who responded to Aslan with fear and hatred swerved away into darkness, and were never seen again. Those who responded with love, even though with fear, entered through the doorway into Aslan's land. The new life was open to all those who recognised Aslan and accepted his lordship of their lives. It didn't mean that they had always been perfect and faithful, since Eustace even recognised a dwarf who had shot at the talking horses. But their response to Aslan when they saw him reflected their true and inner attitudes.

A message of the Bible, which may be uncomfortable but cannot be avoided, is the distinction between those who are accepted, forgiven and saved by God, entering into new life, and those who reject his offer and are lost. Many grapple with the concept of a God who can save but also judge, and this picture from *The Last Battle* may help shed light on this. When the time comes for judgement, the attitudes of our hearts will be revelaed.

A heart for truth in the absence of light

" 'Beloved,' said the Glorious One, 'unless thy desire had been for me thou wouldst not have sought so long and so truly. For all find what they truly seek.' "

The Calormene, Emeth, had sought the truth, as far as he knew it. He had believed in Tash, and thought he was following Tash. But it was apparent that his heart had been hungering after the One who was the Truth. As soon as he saw Aslan, he fell at his feet, recognising that it was better to see Aslan and die than to have everything that the world could offer and not see him.

Did this mean that all gods were the same—Tash and Aslan were one? Absolutely not, says Aslan. Emeth's devotion in the past had been directed at the wrong name, and in the wrong manner, but his heart had been right. He received new life and entered into Aslan's country. Aslan knew his real heart.

God is not looking for people who are concentrating on keeping the right set of rules, but for those who will accept Him for who He is, and willingly accept Him as Lord of their lives.

Some Christian Elements found in Narnia

In the Introduction it was explained that the Chronicles of Narnia were not originally planned as a Christian allegory. However, the purpose of this book has been to help those readers who wish to, to identify some of the Christian elements that C.S. Lewis said "pushed their way into the stories."

The introduction listed a few key Christian themes which run through the books. For those who are not very familiar with the message of the Bible, these are expanded in a little more detail below.

○ The creation of the world, the entry of evil into it, and its final end.

The Bible teaches that the world did not arise spontaneously from nothing, but that there is a Creator who planned the world and made it good. However, evil entered into it, and has been in the hearts of all humans, which is why there is so much evil and suffering in the world. According to the principles of justice, this evil leads to the death of all. The Bible also talks of an end time, when the Creator will bring the world as we know it to a close.

One theme which is assumed in the Bible is that a true recognition of who God is and what He is like should result in both awe and love—awe at his greatness, and a response of attraction, wanting to be part of his magnificent plan.

○ The existence of a Being and His Representative, who cared enough about the world to die for it, but who came alive again, conquering death.

It is made clear throughout the Bible that God had a plan to deliver men and women from the result of the evil in the world and in their hearts. The only way that this was possible, consistent with the just laws on which the world was created, was through the death of an innocent person. Since no such person exists, God chose to come as a human, Jesus, who lived and then died for the world. However, this act resulted in death itself being overcome, and so he came alive again after 3 days. Christians remember this each Easter, as an historical event of about AD 30.

○ The Creator's personal intervention in the lives of individuals.

The teaching of the Bible, both from the time before Jesus' life and the time after, is that God, through Jesus, wants a personal relationship with individuals. The most obvious example of this is prayer. But the relationship must be one that recognises God's greatness.

This aspect of personal relationships with people is apparent throughout the events recorded in the Old Testament (the first part of the Bible) and was expressed most clearly in Jesus' dealings with individuals, as recorded in the New Testament.

○ The need to believe in Him, trust Him and follow Him closely, even at times when He seems distant.

This key Christian theme is that God wants us to trust Him. The experience of people in many different parts of the Bible is that sometimes God might seem remote. A real test of their trust in Him and love for Him was whether they held on in these more difficult times.

It is also made clear in the Bible, that following Jesus will not be easy. It can be a lonely path, making demands that effectively fundamentally change attitudes and lifestyle. The realisation that true life depends on a relationship with God means that priorities shift. The initial act of believing is just the first step on the road of following Christ.

Notes and References

General Reading

1 C.S. Lewis, *Of This and Other Worlds*, edited by Walter Hooper, published by HarperCollins

   This collection of essays by C.S.Lewis includes one entitled *Sometimes Fairy Stories Say Best What's to be Said*, which explains Lewis's thinking behind his own stories.

2 C.S. Lewis, *Surprised by Joy*.

   In this partly auto-biographical book, C.S. Lewis explains how he moved from atheism to Christianity.